Inspirational Poems for Healing

Inspirational Poems for Healing

Felice S.C

All scriptures taken from the lasted KJV and NIV

Text copyright 2024 Felice S.C

Illustrations copyright Felice S.C

All reserved. Published by Right Side Publishing

Please contact the author at the e-mail below for permissions and speaking events.

feliciacauley@ymail.com

Published in the US

Cover design -Zeesha

Rain photo by upslash

Editor Felicia Cauley

Project Manager

Robert Cauley

Inspirational Poems for Healing

ISBN- 978-1-955050-18-0

Library Of Congress Number-2024903892

Acknowledgment

Thank you, Lord, for giving me the idea for this book. I thank my husband, Robert, for listening to my book ideas and staying up with me to keep me company while I write. I thank our divine four, our adult children, Micleicia, John, Johnesha, and Antalicia, for cheering me on through my healing journey. My sisters, Kenyatta, Mary, and Ebonie; brothers, Ronald (Ronnie), Chris, and John, encouraged me to use my gifts. I love you all. May God bless you and heaven shine on you.

Dedication

To everyone suffering from

disease or anguish

Jesus went throughout Galilee, teaching in their synagogues, proclaiming the good news of the kingdom, and healing every disease and sickness among the people.

Matthew 4:23 NIV

Contents

Felice S.C

MUSTARD SEED

In the kingdom of Heaven, it is mentioned,

Faith as small as a mustard seed.

A seed that sprouts from humble ground,

Yet its strength and power know no bounds.

A tiny speck, so easily dismissed,

But within it dwells a truth that persists.

For in this seed, a belief takes root,

A conviction that blossoms, bearing fruit.

Though barren fields may lay before,

A mustard seed holds the promise to soar.

With patience and trust, it perseveres,

Bringing forth hope despite the fears.

For faith is not measured by size or might,

But instead, the courage to hold on tight.

It teaches us that the smallest things,

Can grow into majestic blessings life brings.

Like a mustard seed, let our faith ignite,

A beacon of love in the darkest night.

May we hold onto hope, never to cease,

And spread its light, granting others peace.

So, remember, as you go on your way,

The faith of a mustard seed, I say.

It may seem small, but don't be misled,

For within it lies the strength to be spread.

PAIN

In the depths of despair, when all hope seems lost,

When wounds cut deep and heartache feels exhaust,

There stands a divine antidote to all strife,

A presence, a solace that mends this life.

For there is no pain, however fierce, God can not heal,

No sorrow, however heavy, He can't reveal,

A balm for the broken, a salve for the soul,

He embraces the wounded, their fears He'll console.

With tender compassion, He eases our plight,

Pouring love like a river, day and night,

He reaches out gently, His touch oh so kind,

Eradicating darkness that concealed our mind.

Through tumultuous storms, gentle whispers He'll send,

Nudging us forward, helping us transcend,

For His grace knows no bounds, His mercy profound,

He reignites the embers within us, unbound.

Through trials and tribulations, we face,

He's there, our refuge, our saving grace,

arms wide open, He's always nearby,

To shelter, to guide, to wipe every tear dry.

Though sorrows may linger, and pain may persist,

Faith in His presence, we must never resist,

For in every setback, His purpose remains,

To strengthen our spirit, to heal our deep pains.

So let no despair consume your weary heart,

Let His love envelops from end to start,

For no pain, however daunting, He can't mend,

No sorrow, however crushing, He can't transcend.

LIVE FOR TODAY

Dream but live for today,

Today is all you have right now.

Let go of worries that hold you at bay,

Embrace the present, art thou.

For dreams carry us to distant lands,

On wings of hope and desire.

But don't let tomorrow slip through your hands,

For today is when you light the fire.

Dream of a bright and joyful future,

But savor the beauty of today's sunrise.

Feel the warmth, let it nurture,

Embrace each moment; no need to compromise.

Dreams give us purpose, ambition, and drive,

They guide us through the darkest night.

But let not the present pass us by,

For it's a gift, a treasure, shining so bright.

Plan for tomorrow, envision your dreams,

But live in the now, dance with delight.

Let life unfold with its unpredictable themes,

Cherishing today, from morning till night.

Dream big, but hold today in your heart,

For it's the foundation on which dreams are built.

Embrace the now, let the worries depart,

Awaken your soul, with every moment fulfilled.

Dream but live for today,

Today is all you have right now.

Carpe diem, seize the day,

And let your dreams find their sacred vow.

Embrace the Now

O, who can know what lies beyond this day?

When futures fade and promises are lost,

The present moment holds our only way,

A chance to cherish, no matter the cost.

Amidst the chaos and the fleeting time,

We find our souls yearning for something more,

A sacred connection, divine and sublime,

To lift us up and help us to restore.

Let go of worries that weigh down your heart,

For yesterday's sorrow holds no tomorrow.

In each breath we take, a brand new start,

A chance to heal, to love without sorrow.

live for today, embrace its embrace,

And find solace in this sacred space.

JESUS

Jesus, my Savior, in times of despair,

You pull me close, with love beyond compare.

You heal my wounds, a balm for my soul,

With grace and mercy, You make me whole.

Jesus, my Lord, You guide my way,

Through darkest nights, You're the light of day.

You lift me up, when spirits are low,

With gentle whispers, Your love does show.

Jesus, the cure for all diseases known,

You mend the broken, the pain You've sown.

Your blood, a remedy, stains the cross,

Redeeming all, no matter the .

Jesus, my Redeemer, with arms outstretched,

You paid the price on Calvary'.

Your sacrifice, a gift for us all,

In Your presence, I'll never fear the fall.

You are the Alpha, the Omega too,

Beginning and end, in all that I do.

Jesus, my All, my refuge, and shield,

In Your embrace, my heart is healed.

So, I'll sing Your praises, from dawn 'til night,

To share Your love, and Your glorious light.

Jesus, my Savior, Jesus, my Lord,

In You, I find hope, forever adored.

No room for Rabies, no room at all,

This body is no resting place for you.

In veins that pulse with life, you won't enthrall,

For strength and hope shall see this battle through.

CANCER

Your presence here has no authority,

Your vile whispers shunned by fortitude.

Defiance sings, clad in unity,

The spirit's flame resists, unwavering and shrewd.

Within this vessel, dreams do flourish wild,

With aspirations soaring to the sky.

No darkness shall cloud this vibrant child,

For love and joy shall never be denied.

Though pain may stake its claim in fleeting hours,

The heart holds steadfast, defying your powers.

No room for cancer, no room to reside,

This body fights, refusing to succumb.

Serenade of life and laughter coincide,

As warriors rise, in triumph they become.

Never shall you extinguish this flame bright,

Though you may linger, lurking in the gray.

Hope's beacon shines a beacon of pure light,

Guiding us to a future, cancer-free day.

So leave this sanctuary, cancerous foe,

For here, love's shield protects and in love, we grow.

ON MY KNEES

On my knees in prayer, I'll be,

Seeking solace, my heart set free.

In the quietude of the sacred space,

My spirit finds rest, a heavenly embrace.

With every breath, my soul extends,

A plea for peace, where love transcends.

Through the whispers of humble plea,

In reverence and devotion, I find serenity.

On my knees you see, that is where I'll be,

In fervent surrender, my anxieties flee.

A sanctuary within me, a sacred ground,

Where faith and hope resolutely surround.

With palms open wide, tears may flow,

Yet healing waters within me will grow.

In this humble posture, trust reigns supreme,

Guiding me through life's painful theme.

On my knees, I find strength anew,

A bond with heaven, ever so true.

In surrendering to the Divine's embrace,

Grace floods my being, leaving no trace.

For on these knees, I find humility's charm,

A sanctuary, where love heals and warms.

In prayers whispered from the depths of my soul,

A connection unbreakable, making me whole.

So on my knees in prayer, you'll find me,

For in that sacred act, I am truly free.

Boundless virtues within, entwined so tight,

A testament of faith, casting shadows of light.

LUPUS

Lupus, you have to go, leave this weary frame,

For you invade my sanctuary with ruthless aim.

But know, Lupus, you don't grasp the divine plan,

For God, the ultimate arbitrator, holds the upper hand.

Your presence, so stealthy, has brought anguish and pain,

Testing my spirit, an unwelcome disdain.

But deep within, a steadfast faith I maintain,

That God's mighty sovereignty shall forever reign.

Oh, Lupus, you may deceive with your relentless strife,

But I refuse to surrender, in this battle for life.

For there's a power greater, a healing divine,

A force unmatched, a love that intertwines.

Through the dark tunnels of anguish and despair,

I find solace, knowing God truly cares.

He guides my steps, when weakness resides,

Filling this broken vessel, where hope coincides.

So, Lupus, you must understand your limits,

For God's boundless grace surpasses your gimmicks.

I stand strong, fueled by faith's fervent glow,

Defying your grip, embracing a future's rainbow.

Lupus, with all your might, you'll never comprehend,

The resilience within, a warrior I transcend.

With God's final say an eternal flame aglow,

Bidding you farewell, Lupus, it's time to go.

I CAN'T STAND THE RAIN BUT GOD CAN

In the depths of sorrow, when clouds gather grey,

A restless spirit, burdened by the rain's relentless spray,

I cannot bear the weight of tears that soak my soul,

But in these moments of despair, God's presence takes control.

The skies may weep, cascading droplets like a river's flow,

And in each raindrop, summoned anguish, my heart shall know,

Yet amidst the storms that ravage my fragile being,

God stands firm, an unwavering light, forever foreseeing.

The pain may pierce, like a thousand sharpest thorns,

Leaving scars that ache, where once hope proudly adorned,

But though I stumble in the labyrinth of agony's domain,

God whispers assurance, that He too bears the pain.

For beyond the tempest's fierce embrace, there lies a truth,

That the One who formed the stars, knows the pain of youth,

In every tear that falls and every sorrow that befalls,

God's loving hands shall heal, mending doubts and shattered walls.

I cannot stand the rain, nor endure the depths of despair,

But God, ever merciful, shall carry the burdens I cannot bear,

In His gentle grace, I find solace, hope to reclaim,

For in this vast universe, only God can stand the rain.

FEAR

No more fear,

No matter what I face,

In the quiet spaces where shadows roam,

A heart battles, seeking its way home.

In the hallowed halls of courage, a tale unfolds,

Of a soul adorned with strength, as the story molds.

Fear, a phantom that whispers in the dark,

Yet in the ember of courage, leaves its mark.

A patient, resilient, facing the unknown,

In the battlefield of illness, not alone.

No more fear, let the anthem rise,

A symphony of hope in whispered skies.

For in the realm of struggle, courage stands,

An unwavering fortress, built on faith's sands.

With every labored breath, a testament spoken,

A spirit unbroken, though the body may be broken.

No more fear, a vow etched in the soul,

As the warrior, takes control.

Through the labyrinth of treatment's maze,

The spirit navigates, with a steadfast gaze.

Battles waged in the chambers within,

Yet the courage persists, beneath the skin.

No more fear, for in the darkest night,

There's a flicker of courage, a beacon of light.

God's grace, a balm for wounds unseen,

A force that strengthens, where hope has been.

In the quiet moments of solitude,

The patient finds fortitude.

No more fear, the mantra repeats,

As courage rises from defeat.

The surgeon's scalpel, a wielder of fate,

Yet courage stands firm, refusing to abate.

Chemical warriors coursing through veins,

Yet the patient endures, where strength remains.

No more fear, let the echoes resound,

In the battleground where courage is found.

A dance with uncertainty, a patient's feat,

In God's grace, their solace and heartbeat.

The room may echo with machines' soft hum,

Yet courage reverberates, a powerful drum.

In the sterile air where antiseptics swirl,

A patient's bravery, a flag unfurls.

No more fear, the rallying cry,

As the patient faces the ever-changing sky.

Through valleys of pain and mountains of hope,

In courage's embrace, they learn to cope.

The diagnosis, a storm on the horizon,

Yet courage emerges, a resilient bison.

No more fear, for in the storm's eye,

There's a calm courage, refusing to die.

The loved ones stand as pillars strong,

Their prayers, a chorus, a comforting song.

No more fear, for love surrounds,

A healing force where courage abounds.

In the silence of a hospital room,

Courage blooms, dispelling the gloom.

No more fear, the spirit soars,

As faith opens unseen doors.

Through treatments harsh and side effects dire,

The patient's courage, a blazing fire.

No more fear, as resilience weaves,

A tapestry of strength that never leaves.

The prognosis may paint an uncertain scene,

Yet courage paints hope in shades serene.

No more fear, for the journey's stride,

Is walked with courage by the patient's side.

God's grace, an anchor in the storm,

No more fear, for courage takes form.

In the crucible of illness, a patient refined,

A spirit ablaze, courage enshrined.

So to the patient facing shadows deep,

No more fear, let courage seep.

God's grace, a steadfast sail,

Guiding through every tumultuous gale.

In the tapestry of pain and unknowns,

No more fear, let courage be sown.

For in the heart's quiet, a truth is clear,

In God's grace and courage, no more fear.

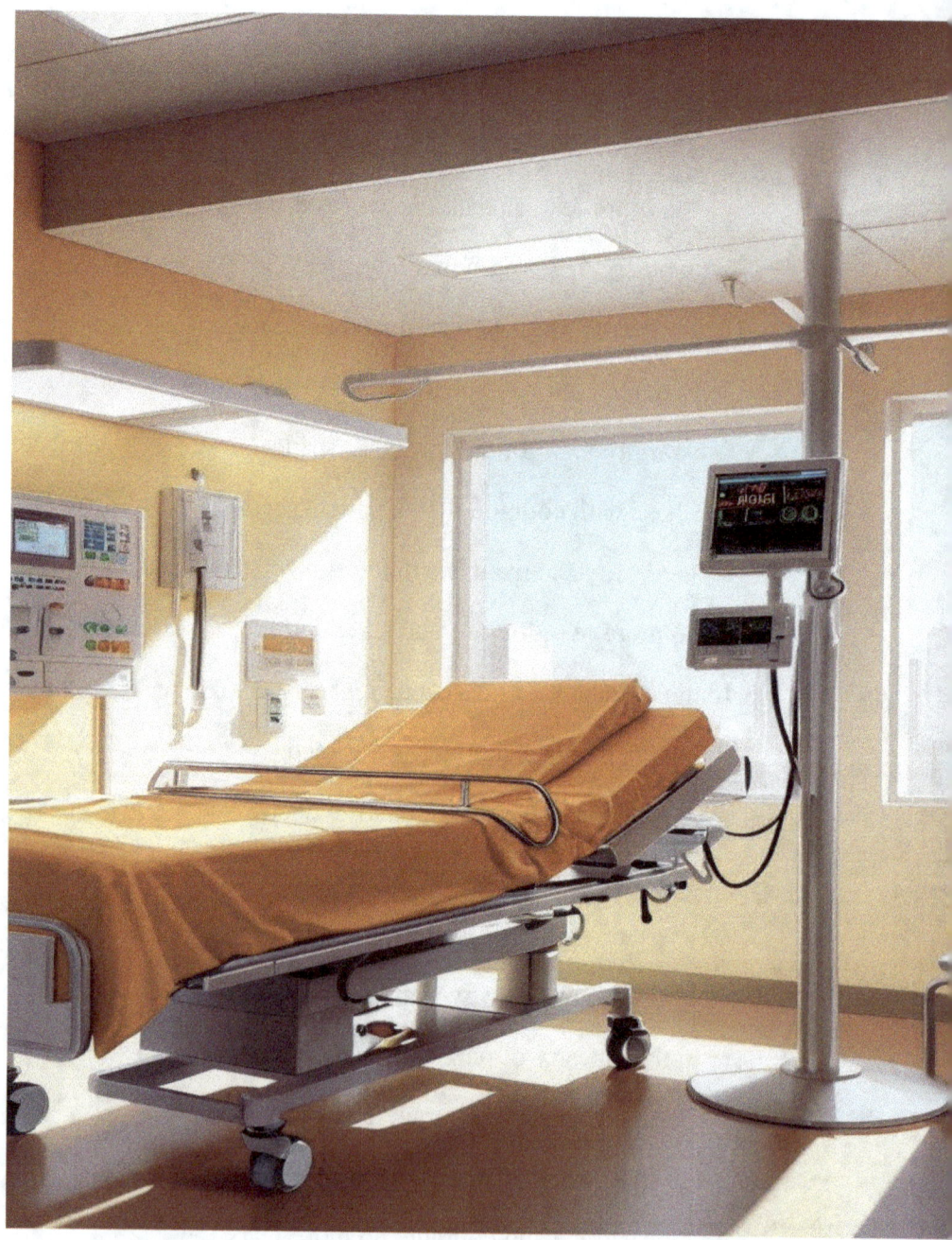

OH THE BEAUTY

Flowers, trees

The sunset

Water, the breeze

In the tapestry of life, where shadows may dance,

A patient emerges in a delicate trance.

Oh, the beauty that whispers in the quiet,

A symphony of nature, a serene riot.

Flowers, in their bloom, tell tales untold,

Of resilience, stories woven in petals bold.

A patient, like a bud, in the garden of strife,

Unfurls with courage, embracing new life.

Each petal, a chapter of the journey unknown,

Yet in the blossom's beauty, strength is shown.

Oh, the beauty that blooms in adversity,

A patient's grace, a poignant diversity.

Trees, with branches reaching for the sky,

Stand tall, echoing the patient's resolute cry.

Rooted in hope, unyielding in the storm,

A patient's spirit, an unwavering form.

The rustling leaves, a melody so sweet,

A symphony of courage, a patient's heartbeat.

Oh, the beauty that sways with the breeze,

A patient's dance, under life's vast trees.

The sunset, a painting of hues divine,

Mirroring the patient's courage, in every line.

As the sun kisses the day goodbye,

A patient finds strength in the painted sky.

A canvas of oranges, pinks, and gold,

A patient's story gracefully told.

Oh, the beauty that fades to the night,

A patient's strength, an eternal light.

Water, a river that flows with grace,

A patient's journey, a gentle embrace.

Through twists and turns, the current strong,

A patient's resilience, a river's song.

The soothing waves, a healing balm,

A patient's calm in the healing psalm.

Oh, the beauty that mirrors in the stream,

A patient's reflection, like a hopeful dream.

The breeze, a whisper in the quiet air,

A patient's courage, beyond compare.

Caressing the face with a gentle touch,

A patient's spirit, a resilient clutch.

Leaves fluttering in the wind's soft kiss,

A patient's journey, in courage, bliss.

Oh, the beauty that dances with the wind,

A patient's strength, in every twirl, pinned.

In the canvas of nature, a patient finds,

A mirror reflecting courageous minds.

Through flowers, trees, and sunsets divine,

Oh, the beauty that makes a patient shine.

So to the one facing the battle's tide,

Let the beauty of nature be your guide.

In every bloom and every breeze,

Find the courage that sets you at ease.

For in the beauty that surrounds us all,

A patient's courage, like a waterfall.

Flowers, trees, the sunset's art,

Reflect the beauty within your heart.

As petals unfold in the morning light,

Embrace the strength that's taking flight.

Like trees standing tall in the wind's embrace,

Feel your roots, find your grace.

With the sunset, let worries fade away,

In the golden hues, let courage sway.

Flow like water in the river's stream,

You're stronger than you may seem.

And in the breeze, hear a whispered song,

A melody of courage, where you belong.

Oh, the beauty that weaves through pain,

In your heart, let resilience reign.

For every petal, every leaf, every ray,

Reflects your courage in its own way.

In the beauty that nature paints so clear,

Find the strength to persevere.

Oh, the beauty that surrounds us all,

In the patient's journey, let courage stand tall.

Amidst the flowers, trees, and skies,

You are a masterpiece in life's endless ties.

LAUGHTER IS GOOD FOR THE SOUL

In the quiet chambers where shadows may dwell,

There is a journey, a tale to tell.

In the midst of illness, a flicker of light,

A simple truth unfolds, a beacon so bright.

Laughter, a melody, pure and free,

A healing balm for the soul, like a gentle sea.

In the echoes of mirth, a patient finds,

Courage and strength that eternally binds.

Through the corridors of sterile white,

Laughter dances, a whimsical sprite.

In the quiet moments, where pain may creep,

In laughter's sweep.

Oh, the beauty that laughter unveils,

In the heart's rhythm, where courage sails.

A medicine potent, laughter's embrace,

A healer of wounds, a comforting grace.

In the humor that dances on lips so brave,

There is courage, a journey to pave.

For in the midst of struggle, when spirits tire,

Laughter kindles a resilient fire.

So let the echoes of laughter resound,

In hospital rooms where strength is found.

In the face of illness, a patient may smile,

For laughter brings joy, even for a while.

In the comedy of life, a patient's stage,

Laughter becomes a powerful sage.

A tonic that soothes, a resilient force,

Guiding a patient on a courageous course.

Through the haze of treatments, the battlefields,

Laughter is the armor that courage wields.

In the face of uncertainty, a patient may find,

Laughter to be the healer, gentle and kind.

In the warmth of shared jokes and funny tales,

Laughter weaves courage in trails.

For the journey though fraught with strife,

Can be adorned with the colors of life.

In the camaraderie of caregivers and friends,

Laughter echoes, a healing amends.

A symphony of joy, a refuge of light,

In laughter's embrace, courage takes flight.

In the humor that rises from the deepest well,

A heart of laughter may quell.

For in the simplicity of a hearty laugh,

Courage unfurls like a vibrant staff.

In the shared chuckles and gleeful cries,

Laughter is the language where courage lies.

Through pain and struggle, a patient may find,

Laughter to be the salve for the mind.

Oh, the beauty that laughter imparts,

A melody that heals broken hearts.

In the canvas of illness, a patient may paint,

Colors of courage, laughter's quaint.

So to the patient facing shadows dark,

Let laughter be your guiding spark.

In the humor that dances in life's grand scroll,

Discover the courage that makes you whole.

In the stories shared with laughter's touch,

Find the strength that you need so much.

For in every giggle, every hearty cheer,

Courage whispers, "There's nothing to fear."

In the comedies of life, find your role,

Let laughter mend, let laughter console.

For in the joyous notes that laughter weaves,

A patient finds courage, a soul that believes.

In the simplicity of a well-timed jest,

A patient's heart finds solace, a nest.

For laughter, like a beacon in the night,

Guides a patient with healing light.

Through the valleys of illness, the peaks of pain,

Laughter becomes a comforting rain.

In its gentle downpour, courage is sown,

A spirit in laughter is known.

So in the face of darkness, let laughter shine,

A resilient star, a courage entwined.

For in the realm of joy, a patient may find,

The strength to endure, the courage to bind.

In the chapters of struggle, let laughter be,

A companion that dances, wild and free.

For in the beauty of mirth, a patient may see,

A courageous soul, resilient and glee.

DANCE, JOY FOR TODAY

In the hallowed halls of the heart, a melody plays,

A song of courage in the patient's gaze.

Dance, oh soul, in the face of strife,

For within the rhythm lies the essence of life.

Dance joy for today, in the whispers of now,

A celebration of life, a solemn vow.

In the echoes of laughter and the steps so light,

I will find courage to take flight.

Hope for tomorrow, in the sunrise of dreams,

A tapestry woven with resilience it seems.

In the dance of shadows and the dawn's sweet kiss,

I will discover courage and eternal bliss.

In the quietude of a hospital room,

Where gloom may linger and shadows loom,

I stand a warrior in grace,

Dancing through challenges, embracing the pace.

Good know-all and see all, the patient may say,

In the dance of faith, guiding the way.

For in the footsteps that mark the floor,

Courage unfolds, an encore.

Today I will dance, in the face of the unknown,

A celebration of strength, a melody sown.

For in the choreography of life's intricate art,

There is a song in my heart.

Dance for life given, a precious gift,

a twirl, as spirits lift.

In the rhythm of breaths, a sacred trance,

Dancing with courage, taking a chance.

Dance for peace within, a tranquil pirouette,

A soul in quiet offset.

For in the stillness, courage is found,

A dancer on life's sacred ground.

Dance for love in my heart, a waltz divine,

love's tendrils entwine.

In the embrace of compassion and care,

Courage blossoms, a dance so rare.

The tune of salvation right from the start,

sways with a courageous heart.

For in the music of life's fleeting chart,

Dance becomes courage, a work of art.

a dancer in the ballroom of fate,

Waltzing through challenges, embracing the weight.

In every turn, every twirl, a story untold,

A dance of courage, a spirit so bold.

Dance joy for today, let the music play,

In the midst of illness, find a brighter day.

For the rhythm of courage, a heartbeat so clear,

Echoes in the dance, banishing fear.

Hope for tomorrow, a waltz in the night,

As I seek the light.

In the dance of dreams and aspirations,

Courage pirouettes, a source of elation.

God know-all and see all, a guiding star,

I will dance no matter how far.

For in the leaps and bounds, courage is found,

A dance that echoes, a resounding sound.

Today I will dance, in the face of despair,

As I sway, defying the wear and tear.

For in the movement, in the graceful glide,

Courage unveils, a patient's pride.

Dance for life given, a celebration so grand,

In the circle of existence, I will stand.

For in the twinkle of every step,

Courage is woven, a fabric so adept.

Dance for peace within, a serene ballet,

As I pirouette through night and day.

For in the still moments, where shadows part,

Courage is kindled, a patient's heart.

Dance for love in your heart, a tango so sweet,

love's rhythm to meet.

In the embrace of empathy and grace,

Courage takes center stage, as I embrace.

The tune of salvation right from the start,

I dance with a courageous heart.

In the symphony of life, where melodies dart,

Courage is the dance, the work of art.

So let the music play, let the me twirl,

In the dance of courage, a resilient whirl.

For in every movement, every tender arc,

Courage is the dancer, leaving a mark.

Dance joy for today, hope for tomorrow,

In the dance of courage, banish sorrow.

For I am a dancer in life's grand mart,

Dancing with courage, a masterpiece of the heart.

Peace

Peace can only be found in the masters hand

In the quiet corridors where courage may wane,

A patient stands, bearing the weight of the pain.

Yet in the stillness, where shadows may creep,

A solace is sought, a promise to keep.

Peace, a delicate whisper in the hush,

A refuge sought in the heart's sacred brush.

In the master's hand, where serenity weaves,

A patient finds courage, as hope conceives.

No battlefield is ever fought in vain,

For in the midst of struggle, peace may reign.

In the dance of cells, where illness may roam,

A patient discovers a sanctuary, a place called home.

Peace can only be found in the master's hand,

A balm for the spirit, where courage may stand.

In the tapestry of suffering, a patient may find,

The touch of peace, a comfort so kind.

Through the corridors of uncertainty and despair,

A patient seeks solace, a healing air.

For in the gentle strokes of the master's hand,

Peace unfolds, a grace so grand.

In the silence that echoes in the hospital room,

A patient finds stillness, like a rose in bloom.

For in the master's hand, where love takes command,

Peace becomes courage, a guiding strand.

A diagnosis, a storm on the horizon,

Yet in the master's hand, hope may arise.

For peace is not absence of struggle, you see,

It's the presence of courage, resilience, and glee.

Through the veins where the battle may rage,

A patient finds peace, turning the page.

In the master's hand, where grace is bestowed,

Courage emerges, a triumphant ode.

The weight of illness, a formidable load,

Yet in the master's hand, courage is stowed.

For peace is not elusive, nor a distant shore,

It's a gentle tide, embracing evermore.

No matter the prognosis, the shadows cast,

In the master's hand, courage holds fast.

For peace is a melody, a harmonious song,

A patient dances with courage, brave and strong.

Through treatments harsh and the body's lament,

In the master's hand, peace is sent.

For the soul that seeks refuge, weary and worn,

Peace becomes the balm, in the master's morn.

Peace can only be found in the master's hand,

A sanctuary in which courage may stand.

In the intricate pattern of trials faced,

A patient discovers a divine embrace.

With every needle pricked and every ache,

In the master's hand, peace does not forsake.

For peace is a journey, a compass so true,

Guiding a patient through skies so blue.

In the silent whispers of the master's grace,

A patient finds courage in the sacred space.

For peace is a sanctuary, an anchor so deep,

Where the soul finds solace, in the master's keep.

Through the valleys of treatment, where shadows cast,

A patient walks with peace, steadfast.

For in the master's hand, where love intertwines,

Courage blossoms, and hope shines.

Peace can only be found in the master's hand,

A beacon in the darkness, where courage may stand.

In the mosaic of pain and the palette of fears,

A patient paints with peace, wiping away tears.

As the body battles and the spirit contends,

In the master's hand, peace descends.

For peace is not absence of turmoil and strife,

It's the presence of courage, the essence of life.

Through the nights of worry and the days of doubt,

In the master's hand, peace is devout.

For in the gentle cradle of divine love,

A patient finds peace, soaring above.

Peace can only be found in the master's hand,

A melody of solace, sweeping the land.

In the intricate dance of courage and pain,

A patient discovers peace is not in vain.

With every breath, in the stillness so grand,

A patient finds peace, crafted by the master's hand.

For in the midst of turmoil, where shadows command,

Courage is kindled, as peace takes a stand.

STANDING

Standing on God's promises

In the quiet chambers where shadows may dwell,

When you stand, in the fortress of courage, so well.

Standing on God's promises, a resolute soul,

In the face of illness, seeking to be whole.

With every heartbeat, a rhythm so strong,

You can stand where faith belongs.

In the crucible of sickness, a steadfast decree,

Standing on God's promises, courage set free.

No armor of steel, no shield so grand,

You stand, firm on God's hand.

In the tapestry of struggle, where pain may weave,

Standing on promises, a spirit won't deceive.

Standing on God's promises, a mantra so pure,

In the echo of prayers, courage shall endure.

For promises spoken, in the sacred morn,

Guide a patient's steps, a hope reborn.

In the labyrinth of treatments, where uncertainty may reign, you stand in faith's gentle terrain.

Standing on God's promises, an anchor in the storm,

For in every challenge, a patient transform.

Through the maze of diagnoses, where shadows may creep,

You stand, in the promises, so deep.

For God's words echo, like a timeless rhyme,

In the corridors of courage, transcending time.

Standing on God's promises, a beacon so bright,

In the darkest hours, a patient's resolute light.

For promises spoken, a celestial bond,

you stand in God's grace, so fond.

With every medication, every trial faced,

Stand in God's embrace,

Standing on promises, a fortress so grand,

In the palm of His hand, courage takes a stand.

Through the needles and scans, where fear may reside,

you stand, in God's promises, a guide.

For in every setback, every hurdle embraced,

Standing on God's promises, courage retraced.

Standing on God's promises, like mountains so tall,

you stand, refusing to fall.

For promises echo, in the valleys below,

you stand, with courage aglow.

In the silent prayers whispered at night,

You stand, in God's reassuring light.

Standing on promises, a hymn so sweet,

In the melody of courage your heartbeat.

Through the side effects and the weariness profound,

you stand on God's promises, unbound.

For in the storm's fury, and the winds that may blow,

Standing on promises, you shall grow.

Standing on God's promises, a celestial vow,

In the uncertain moments, courage shall plough.

For promises are eternal, a beacon so clear,

You stand in the realm of no fear.

With every tear shed and every smile worn,

You stand, in the promises, reborn.

For God's love is steadfast, a comforting shore,

In the dance of courage, you shall soar.

Standing on God's promises, a melody divine,

In the heart's symphony, courage intertwines,

For promises are whispers in the silent night,

You stand, embracing the light.

In the waiting rooms and the moments of despair,

You stand, in God's promises rare.

For the journey is long, and the path may be steep,

Standing on promises you take the leap.

Standing on God's promises, a truth so pure,

In the tapestry of faith, courage shall endure.

For promises spoken you believe,

In the sanctuary of hope, where courage conceives.

Through the sleepless nights and the ache within,

You stand, in the promises akin.

For God's words resonate, a gentle refrain,

In the cadence of courage, you gain.

Standing on God's promises, a sacred ground,

In the silence profound, courage is found.

For promises spoken, like a sacred decree,

You stand, with a heart so free.

With every step forward, and every setback faced,

You stand, in the promises embraced.

For God's grace is boundless, like the endless sea,

In the symphony of courage, you find glee.

in the face of illness, where shadows may fall,

You stand on God's promises tall.

For promises spoken, in whispers so grand,

You stand, guided by God's hand.

TUNE-UP

THIS BODY

In the quiet symphony of a hospital room,

A patient awaits, facing the impending gloom.

Yet amidst the beeping monitors and hushed whispers,

Hope emerges, as courage lingers.

This body, a vessel in the dance of fate,

Navigating the rhythm of a medical state.

With every beep and hum, a tune unfolds,

A melody of courage, a story untold.

This body, a canvas painted with scars,

Yet within its tapestry, hope's light stars.

For in the quiet tune-up, where healing may start,

A patient finds courage, a resilient heart.

In the hands of caregivers, like skilled musicians,

This body undergoes a healing rendition.

With precision and care, like a skilled conductor,

Hope orchestrates a courageous counter.

This body, a composition of cells and dreams,

In the tune-up of life, resilience gleams.

With every medication, every intervention,

A patient finds strength, defying convention.

The tune-up begins with the first ray of light,

As morning whispers hope, banishing the night.

In the corridors of hospitals, where shadows may creep,

This body finds courage in the tune-up's sweep.

With every needle prick, every medication's dose,

This body stands firm, courage engrossed.

For in the tune-up's process, a patient may find,

A symphony of strength, beautifully designed.

This body, an instrument in the hands of care,

Undergoing a tune-up, a journey rare.

In the operating rooms and chemotherapy's chair,

A patient finds courage, a melody to bear.

Tune-up the cells, the organs, and the soul,

In the healing process, courage takes control.

With each surgical incision and every medication's grace,

This body stands strong, in the tune-up's embrace.

The tune-up is not just a medical ritual,

But a sacred dance of courage, so pivotal.

In the face of illness, where shadows loom,

This body finds strength in the tune-up room.

This body, like a piano with keys so frail,

Yet in the tune-up, resilience sets sail.

For every note played, every chord struck,

Courage reverberates, in the tune-up's luck.

Tune-up the spirits, tune-up the hope,

In the patient's journey, courage shall cope.

With every scan and every therapy's start,

This body dances with courage, a work of art.

This body, like a violin in a healer's hand,

In the tune-up process, hope is planned.

With the strokes of compassion, the notes of care,

Courage harmonizes, filling the air.

Tune-up the mindset, the outlook, the view,

In the patient's journey, courage shines through.

With every supportive word and every caring touch,

This body finds strength, courage in clutch.

This body, like a symphony in a healing song,

In the tune-up's embrace, courage belongs.

With the dedication of healthcare's skilled crew,

Hope orchestrates a courageous breakthrough.

Tune-up the fears, the doubts, the pain,

In the melody of healing, courage shall reign.

With every treatment endured, every test faced,

This body stands tall, courage encased.

This body, like a drum in a heartbeat's rhyme,

In the tune-up's cadence, courage climbs.

With every step forward, every setback met,

This body finds courage, a resilient bet.

Tune-up the resilience, the fight, the will,

In the patient's journey, courage spills.

With every heartbeat and every breath,

This body stands strong, defying death.

This body, like a choir in a healing hymn,

In the tune-up's embrace, courage begins.

With every prayer uttered, every hope held,

This body finds strength, courage compelled.

Tune-up the emotions, the highs, the lows,

In the patient's journey, courage grows.

With every tear shed and every smile worn,

This body dances with courage, reborn.

This body, a masterpiece in the tune-up's play,

In the healing symphony, courage stays.

With every treatment plan and every road ahead,

This body stands courageous, no longer misled.

Tune-up the spirit, the essence, the core,

In the patient's journey, courage implores.

With every heartbeat, every soulful breath,

This body finds courage, conquering death.

In the symphony of healing, where courage is the theme,

This body stands resilient, a triumphant dream.

With every note played and every chord struck,

Courage echoes in the tune-up's luck.

MUSIC

Music is freeing, smoothing, and relieving,

In the hushed corridors where shadows may linger,

Strength may wither.

Yet, in the quietude, where the stillness resides,

A melody unfolds, where hope abides.

Music, a healer is in the room,

A soothing balm, a comfort that will loom.

In the notes that dance, in the rhythms' embrace,

a resilient grace.

Music is freeing, a salve for the soul,

In the journey of illness, where shadows take toll.

With every chord played and every lyric sung,

The spirit is lifted, courage begun.

In the symphony of treatment and recovery,

Music becomes a companion, a source of discovery.

With every melody, every harmonious thread,

A you find faith where strength is bred.

The soft piano keys, like gentle rain,

Compose a melody, soothing the pain.

In the patient's heart, where courage may sway,

Music brings solace, in the healing array.

Music is smoothing, like a cool breeze,

In the scorching heat of disease.

With every lyric that resonates, every rhythm that flows,

Faith and melody grow.

The strumming of a guitar, like a heartbeat strong,

This is a journey where courage belongs.

With every note that reverberates, every tune that plays,

Music becomes courage, in myriad ways.

In the melody's cadence, where silence recedes,

stand strong and exceeds.

For in the composition of hope, where music is key,

Strength unfolds, like waves in the sea.

Music is relieving, a remedy rare,

In the moments of pain, in despair.

With every song that whispers, every tune that consoles,

There is hope where resilience strolls.

The violin's lament, like tears softly shed,

In the heart where courage is bred.

With every bow stroke, every melancholy strain,

Music becomes courage, a refuge in the rain.

Music is freeing, a flight for the soul,

In the journey, where shadows may stroll.

With every melody, every harmonious sound,

strength unbound.

The beat of a drum, like a heartbeat true,

In your chest, faith accrues.

With every rhythmic pulse, every percussive beat,

Music becomes courage, a dance in defeat.

The flute's sweet whisper, like a breeze so light,

In the spirit, where faith takes flight.

With every airy note, every ethereal tone,

Music becomes strength, a comfort zone.

In the harmony of voices, like a choir's embrace,

In the soul, peace finds its place.

With every unified hymn, every choral decree,

Music becomes peace, a symphony free.

The saxophone's wail, like a soulful cry,

In the heart, where peace lies.

With every passionate riff, every jazzy refrain,

Music becomes a powerful gain.

Music is freeing, smoothing, and relieving,

where hope is achieving.

With every note that cascades, every chord that weaves,

Music becomes hope, as you believe.

In the composition of courage, where melodies sway,

Stands strong, in the healing array.

With every musical note, every harmonious strand,

Music becomes courage, a guiding hand.

So, in the quiet moments where shadows may roam,

Let music be a companion, a hope totem.

With every song that echoes, every melody spun,

Music becomes courage, a resilient sonnet unsung.

COME THROUGH JESUS

In the sacred spaces where prayers ascend,

A patient seeks solace around the bend.

In the realm of illness, where shadows play,

A plea echoes softly, "Come through, Jesus, today."

Through the corridors of uncertainty and fear,

A patient stands, with faith sincere.

In the dance of diagnosis, where the unknown weaves,

A heart whispers, "Come through, Jesus,

in grace that relieves."

Come through, Jesus, in the doctor's report,

When the news is heavy, it is a burden to escort.

In the language of numbers, in charts that unfold,

Come through, Jesus, let your healing be told.

In the sterile rooms, where treatments commence,

A patient yearns for a divine presence.

Through the needles and scans, where anxiety resides,

Come through, Jesus, be the light that guides.

In the waiting rooms, where time is weighed,

A patient prays, in the shadows' shade.

In the quiet moments, where doubts may brew,

Come through, Jesus, be the strength anew.

Come through, Jesus, in the darkest night,

When the pain is sharp and steals delight.

In the silence where tears may flow,

Come through, Jesus, let your love bestow.

Through the chemotherapy's relentless storm,

A patient dreams of a healing form.

In the battle within, where courage is strained,

Come through, Jesus, in victory gained.

Come through, Jesus, in the surgeon's hand,

When scalpels dance as a healing band.

In the operating room, where hope may fray,

Come through, Jesus, light the way.

In the embrace of family, in the warmth of a friend,

A patient seeks solace around every bend.

Come through, Jesus, in the touch of care,

Be the answer to the whispered prayer.

Through the scans that map the body's fight,

A patient yearns for a glimmer of light.

In the beeping monitors, where life's measured pulse,

Come through, Jesus, let faith convulse.

Come through, Jesus, in the echo of pain,

When the body's plea is a silent refrain.

In the recesses of suffering, where courage is tested,

Come through, Jesus, in the heart's nested.

In the moments of despair, when hope is frail,

A patient calls out, with a voice so frail.

Come through, Jesus, be the calm in the storm,

In the healing embrace, let courage transform.

Come through, Jesus, in the support that surrounds,

When love and prayers form resilient bounds.

In the hands of caregivers, with skills profound,

Come through, Jesus, in every healing sound.

In the prayers whispered at the break of day,

A patient seeks strength along the way.

Come through, Jesus, be the anchor firm,

In the tides of illness, let courage affirm.

Come through, Jesus, in the laughter's light,

When joy is medicine, a healing sight.

In the moments of respite, where spirits lift,

Come through, Jesus, be the soothing gift.

Through the nights of weariness,

where dreams may falter,

A patient dreams of a grace to alter.

Come through, Jesus, in the quiet of rest,

Be the peace that holds, the soul's bequest.

In the love that lingers, in the memories shared,

A patient finds solace, in the moments paired.

Come through, Jesus, in bonds unbroken,

In the healing journey, be the unspoken.

Come through, Jesus, in the triumphs small,

When victories echo through the hospital hall.

In the steps toward healing, where progress is shown,

Come through, Jesus, in victories unknown.

Through the weary steps of the uphill climb,

A patient seeks strength in faith sublime.

Come through, Jesus, in the uphill race,

Be the endurance, the patient's grace.

Come through, Jesus, in the quiet reflection,

When the spirit finds a peaceful connection.

In the whispered gratitude, where courage is heard,

Come through, Jesus, in every healing word.

Through the valleys of despair,

where shadows may play,

A patient longs for dawn's hopeful ray.

Come through, Jesus, in the dawn's soft hue,

Be the promise of a day anew.

In the resilience that rises from ashes,

A patient seeks courage in life's clashes.

Come through, Jesus, in the phoenix's flight,

Be the resurrection, the patient's light.

Through the ebb and flow of the healing tide,

A patient dreams with arms open wide.

Come through, Jesus, in the waves that roll,

Be the healer, the courageous soul.

Come through, Jesus, in the songs of praise,

When the heart's anthem is a healing phase.

In the hymns of faith, where hope is sung,

Come through, Jesus, in every healing tongue.

In the communion of souls, where love prevails,

A patient finds strength in faith's details.

Come through, Jesus, in the communion's grace,

Be the warmth that transcends every space.

Through the pages of the journey's book,

A patient yearns for a healing look.

Come through, Jesus, in the story told,

Be the narrative of courage unfold.

Come through, Jesus, in the whispers of the wind,

When hope is a melody, softly thinned.

In the gentle breeze that cradles the soul,

Come through, Jesus, be the courage, the ultimate goal.

So, in the echo of prayers, in the quiet plea,

A patient calls out, "Come through, Jesus, be with me."

In the healing journey, where courage is a must,

May Jesus come through, in love and in trust.

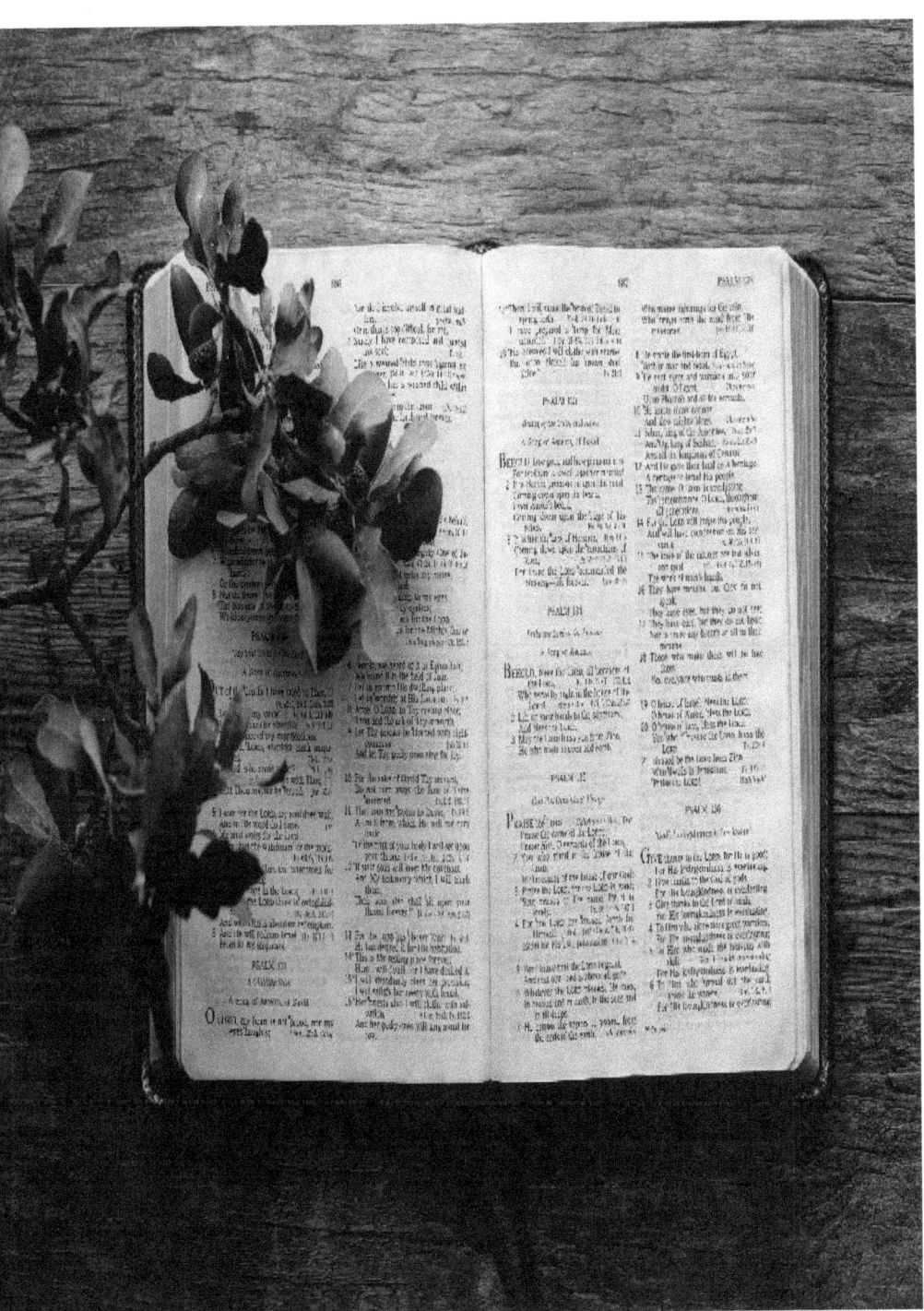

Brighter days are ahead

In the realm of shadows, where illness may reside,

A patient stands, courage as a guide.

Amidst the echoes of uncertainty and fear,

A whisper resounds, "Brighter days are near."

Brighter days are ahead, a mantra to hold,

In the tapestry of challenges, courage unfolds.

Through the corridors of treatment, where shadows loom,

A patient finds solace, in hope's gentle bloom.

In the quiet moments, where tears may fall,

A patient stands tall, amidst the pall.

For in despair, where courage wades,

Brighter days are promised, in healing cascades.

Brighter days are ahead, like the morning's light,

Dispelling the darkness that veils the night.

Through the chemotherapy's storm and the surgeon's knife,

A patient believes in the promise of life.

In the silent prayers uttered, where hope takes flight,

Brighter days emerge, like stars in the night.

Through the weariness and the nights so long,

A patient finds courage in the hope song.

Brighter days are ahead, in the laughter's sound,

A symphony of joy, where healing is found.

Through the challenges that may seem too steep,

A patient stands firm, in courage to leap.

In the warmth of friendships and family near,

Brighter days beckon, dispelling the fear.

Through the support that embraces like a gentle tide,

A patient discovers courage, in love's wide.

Brighter days are ahead, like a canvas blank,

A patient paints courage, a vivid thank.

Through the pain and the struggle to endure,

A patient finds strength, in courage pure.

In the resilience that rises from despair,

Brighter days unfold, a victory to declare.

Through the moments of doubt and shadows cast,

A patient clings to courage, in faith steadfast.

Brighter days are ahead, like a horizon clear,

A patient envisions, overcoming fear.

Through the valleys and peaks of the healing quest,

A patient believes in courage's best.

In the echoes of hope that linger and stay,

Brighter days emerge, chasing shadows away.

Through the tests faced and the mountains climbed,

A patient strides forward, courage enshrined.

Brighter days are ahead, in the dreams untold,

A patient embraces them, courage to hold.

Through the uncertainties that may linger still,

A patient persists, in courage's thrill.

In the whispers of encouragement that grace the air,

Brighter days beckon, a promise to declare.

Through the resilience that refuses to yield,

A patient stands courageous, in hope's field.

Brighter days are ahead, a beacon so bright,

A patient journeys towards them, in courage's light.

Through the stormy seas and the winds that may blow,

A patient sails forth, in courage's flow.

In the quiet moments of reflection and grace,

Brighter days are glimpsed, a hopeful embrace.

Through the scars and the battles fought,

A patient emerges, with courage fraught.

Brighter days are ahead, in the sunrise so grand,

A patient believes in hope's command.

Through the darkest nights and the trials faced,

A patient discovers courage, beautifully laced.

In the heart's symphony, where courage plays,

Brighter days resonate, in hope's arrays.

Through the journey of healing,

where shadows may part,

A patient walks onward,

with courage as heart.

STAND IN THE FIGHT

In the battlefield of illness, where shadows loom,

You stand facing a journey of gloom.

Yet in the heart's fortress, where courage ignites,

A resolute spirit emerges, ready to fight.

Stand in the fight, a rallying cry,

Against the odds, beneath the daunting sky.

In the corridors of hospitals, where whispers abound,

You can stand strong, on courage's ground.

In the sterile rooms, where needles pierce,

You will find strength, facing the fierce.

Against the invaders, the cells gone astray,

Stand in the fight, with courage to sway.

Through the scans that map the unseen strife,

Stands firm, embracing life.

In the face of diagnoses, where fears collide,

Stay in the fight, with Christ as a guide.

In the chemotherapy's storm, where weakness may surge,

stand resilient, a courageous urge.

Against the tides of nausea, the fatigue's might,

Stand in the fight, with unwavering light.

In the surgeon's hands, where healing may start,

stand trusting, in God with all your heart.

Against the incisions and the scars, they bestow,

Stand in the fight, with resilience to show.

Through the uncertainties, where questions persist,

Stand strong in the fight to resist.

In the labyrinth of treatments, where paths entwine,

Stand in the fight, with a spirit divine.

In the waiting rooms, where time ticks slow,

stands patient for you know God is with you

Against the anxiety that lingers near,

Stand in the fight, with courage sincere.

Through the support of loved ones, a fortress so grand,

stand fortified, in the faith band.

In the hands of caregivers, with skills profound,

Stand in the fight, with grace abound.

Against the fears that silently creep,

A God stands watchful, you he will keep.

In the solitude of reflection, where doubts may play,

Stand in the fight, with courage each day.

Through the nights of weariness, where dreams may falter,

stand resilient with no courageous alter.

Against the darkness that threatens to sway,

Stand in the fight, with your faith at bay.

In the echoes of prayers, where hope takes flight,

You stand faithfully, in the fight.

Against the shadows that may seek to confound,

Stand in the fight, with strength unbound.

Through the valleys of despair, where tears may flow,

stand sturdy, and your faith will show.

In the symphony of pain, where the melody's blight,

Stand in the fight, with courage so bright.

Against the setbacks and the setbacks anew,

You stand tenaciously with hope in view.

In the ebb and flow of the healing tide,

Stand in the fight, with courage as guide.

Through the highs and lows, where emotions may sway,

Keep standing resilient with courage to convey.

Against the uncertainty that shrouds the sight,

Stand in the fight, with courage as light.

In the laughter that echoes, a medicine so sweet,

You will stand joyfully with courage replete.

Against the heaviness that illness may brew,

Stand in the fight, with courage anew.

Through the moments of respite, where spirits lift,

Youi will stand hopeful, courage to sift.

In the dance with joy, where moments ignite,

Stand in the fight, with courage in flight.

Against the whispers of doubt, where shadows may tease,

You stand confidently and seize.

In the conviction that carries through the night,

Stand in the fight, with courage so bright.

Through the weariness of battles, where victories are sought,

triumphant, courage uncaught.

Against the echoes of pain that may bite,

Stand in the fight, with hope in sight.

In the camaraderie with fellow warriors so bold,

You stand united with God to hold.

Against the solitude that may threaten to smite,

Stand in the fight, with healing strife.

Through the wear and tear of the body's frame,

You stand on courage to claim.

In the perseverance that defines the might,

Stand in the fight, with courage alight.

Against the whispers of fear that may persist,

You stand undeterred as Christ to enlist.

In the battlefield of illness, where shadows alight,

Stand in the fight, with hope so bright.

Through the tests faced and the mountains to climb,

stand steadfast, God in prime.

Against the doubts that may seek to incite,

Stand in the fight, with Jesus in flight.

In the dreams that persist, where hope takes root,

stand determined, courage to reboot.

Against the odds, where darkness may smite,

Stand in the fight, with God as the light.

Through the journey of healing, where paths intertwine,

You stand resilient, courage to define.

In the resilience that rises from the night,

Stand in the fight, with courage so bright.

Against the whispers of surrender that may beckon,

stand firm, peace as a weapon.

In the symphony of strength, where melodies unite,

Stand in the fight, with courage so bright.

Through the pages of the healing story yet to unfold,

stand hopeful, courage to hold.

Against the unknown that may incite,

Stand in the fight, with courage alight.

In the quiet moments where prayers may resound,

stand anchored, courage profound.

Against the uncertainties, where shadows may write,

Stand in the fight, with courage so bright.

Through the resilience that defines the soul's core,

stand undefeated, faith to adore.

In the triumphs and setbacks alike,

Stand in the fight, a warrior to strike.

Against the echoes of pain that may persist,

stand relentlessly to insist,

In the battle of healing, where courage takes flight,

Stand in the fight, with unwavering light.

TRUST THE MAN WHO WALKED ON WATER AND CALMED THE SEA

In the depths of uncertainty, where shadows may play,

A patient stands, facing a daunting array.

Yet in the heart's refuge, where courage takes hold,

Trust the man who walked on water, whose stories are told.

In the quiet moments of solitude and strife,

A patient seeks solace in the tapestry of life.

Through the corridors of diagnosis, where fears may accrue,

Trust the man who walked on water, for His grace is true.

In the hushed conversations between doctor and kin,

A patient yearns for a healing within.

Through the echoes of prognosis, where uncertainties breed,

Trust the man who walked on water, in His love take heed.

In the sterile rooms where treatments unfold,

A patient finds strength, in the stories of old.

Through the needles and scans, where anxieties climb,

Trust the man who walked on water, for He transcends time.

In the waiting rooms, where time seems to pause,

A patient longs for hope, in the healing cause.

Through the quietude of reflection, where doubts may spin,

Trust the man who walked on water, His peace within.

In the chemotherapy's storm, where weakness may rage,

A patient endures, seeking a healing stage.

Through the nausea and fatigue, where shadows may plea,

Trust the man who walked on water, calming the sea.

In the surgeon's hands, where incisions are made,

A patient trusts, in the price to be paid.

Through the scars that mark the healing spree,

Trust the man who walked on water, for He sets free.

In the moments of despair, where pain takes its stand,

A patient looks to the heavens, seeking a helping hand.

Through the agony that threatens to be,

Trust the man who walked on water, to set you free.

In the communion of family, where love intertwines,

A patient finds solace, where healing aligns.

Through the bond that family and faith decree,

Trust the man who walked on water, for His love is the key.

In the hands of caregivers, where skills unfold,

A patient sees kindness, a treasure untold.

Through the compassion that transcends degree,

Trust the man who walked on water, for His mercy to see.

In the laughter that echoes, like a healing song,

A patient discovers joy, resilient and strength.

Through the struggles and moments of glee,

Trust the man who walked on water, for His grace to plea.

In the quiet prayers whispered at the break of dawn,

A patient seeks strength, a new day drawn.

Through the silence that envelopes, where faith may decree,

Trust the man who walked on water, for His presence to see.

In the echoes of support, where friends rally near,

A patient finds comfort, in the bonds so dear.

Through the camaraderie that friendship agrees,

Trust the man who walked on water, for His love to appease.

In the resilience that rises from the darkest night,

A patient stands strong, in courage's light.

Through the trials that the journey may decree,

Trust the man who walked on water, for His love to set you free.

In the highs and lows, where emotions may sway,

A patient holds on, courage to convey.

Through the moments of triumph and the shadows' plea,

Trust the man who walked on water, for His love to guarantee.

Felice S.C

In the echoes of hope that linger and stay,

A patient stands hopefully chasing shadows away.

Through the journey of healing, where courage is the key,

Trust the man who walked on water, for His love to decree.

So, in the midst of the storm and the sea's relentless swell,

A patient trusts in the stories of old to tell.

Through the tumultuous waves, where faith is the plea,

Trust the man who walked on water, for His love to set you free.

DREAM BUT LIVE FOR TODAY

Dream but live for today,

Dream but live for today, a mantra to embrace,

In the journey of healing, through time and space.

where shadows may loom,

find strength, in the present's bloom.

In the quiet moments, where reflections are spun,

Dream but live for today, until the battles are won.,

in the sunlight's ray.

Dream but live for today, like the morning's light,

Be hopeful, against the shadows' might.,

Dream but live for today,

Through the scars that mark the journey's fray,

Dream but live for today, in resilience's display.

Dream but live for today, in the laughter's sound,

cherish joy, where healing is found.

Through the moments of respite, where spirits lift,

Dream but live for today, in the present's gift.

In the waiting rooms, where time seems to slow,

dreams of tomorrow, a hope to sow.

Through the quietude of reflection, where strength may lay,

Dream but live for today, in the courage's bay.

Dream but live for today, in the support so grand,

fortified, hand in hand.

Through the love of family and friends' array,

Dream but live for today, in the bonds that stay.

In the waves, where emotions may ride,

a healing tide,

Dream but live for today, in the hope's display.

Dream but live for today, in the prayers resound,

seeks solace, where grace is found.

Through the silence of supplication, where faith may weigh,

Dream but live for today, in the courage's array.

In the communion of souls, where love takes flight,

dreams of unity, so bright.

Through the bonds that friendship and faith convey,

Dream but live for today, in the heart's display.

Dream but live for today, in the highs and lows,

embraces the courage that courage bestows.

Through the valleys and peaks where emotions may sway,

Dream but live for today, in resilience's array.

In the echoes of support, where loved ones surround,

dreams of healing, where strength is found.

Through the camaraderie that uplifts the fray,

Dream but live for today, I say,

Dream but live for today, in the laughter's sound,

treasures the joy that echoes around.

Through the moments of respite, where spirits lift,

Dream but live for today, in the present's gift.

In the quiet moments of gratitude and grace,

Through the uncertainties that may threaten to sway,

Dream but live for today, tomorrow is not promised.

Live in the present's array.

In the shadows of the unknown, faith is born,

dream of resilience, in the early morn.

Through the tapestry of time, where dreams may convey,

Dream but live for today, in courage's array.

STAY IN THE FIGHT
THROUGH THE TEARS AND PAIN

In the arena of battles, where tears may fall like rain,

A patient stands, facing the storm with courage to regain.

Through the tumultuous journey, where shadows may wane,

Stay in the fight through the tears and pain.

Stay in the fight, a beacon in the night,

Against the adversities, where hope takes flight.

In the corridors of illness, where fears may reign,

A patient finds strength, in courage's terrain.

Through the diagnosis, where uncertainties unfold,

Stay in the fight, let courage be your stronghold.

In the echoes of prognosis, where doubts may stain,

A patient embraces resilience, in the fight to maintain.

Stay in the fight, through the chemotherapy's toll,

A patient endures, with a courageous soul.

In the waves of nausea and fatigue's disdain,

Courage becomes a lifeline, a steadfast chain.

Through the surgeon's hands, where healing may commence,

Stay in the fight, with unwavering confidence.

In the scars that mark the battle's strain,

A patient finds power, in courage to sustain.

Stay in the fight, through the weariness of the quest,

A patient persists, knowing they are blessed.

In the moments of darkness, where shadows disdain,

Courage becomes a guiding light, refusing to wane.

Through the waiting rooms, where time ticks slow,

Stay in the fight, let resilience grow.

In the solitude of reflection, where doubts may feign,

A patient discovers strength, in courage's reign.

Stay in the fight, through the tests and trials,

A patient endures, embracing the miles.

In the symphony of pain, where melodies strain,

Courage becomes a melody, a song to sustain.

Through the camaraderie with loved ones so dear,

Stay in the fight, let the bonds appear.

In the hands of caregivers, where compassion will rain,

Courage becomes a refuge, soothing the pain.

Stay in the fight, through the laughter's sound,

A patient cherishes joy, where healing is found.

In the moments of respite, where spirits regain,

Courage becomes a dance, a rhythm to maintain.

Through the echoes of support that surround,

Stay in the fight, let love abound.

In the communion of souls, where unity is the gain,

Courage becomes a fortress, against the strain.

Stay in the fight, through the highs and lows,

A patient embraces the courage that courage bestows.

In the valleys and peaks, where emotions may strain,

Courage becomes a mountain, unshaken by the rain.

Through the moments of gratitude and grace,

Stay in the fight, let hope embrace.

In the resilience that rises from the pain,

Courage becomes a phoenix, rising once again.

Stay in the fight, through the tears that may flow,

A patient stands tall, letting courage grow.

In the tapestry of struggles, where resilience is ingrained,

Courage becomes a legacy, forever sustained.

Through the nights of weariness, where dreams may fade,

Stay in the fight, let hope cascade.

In the quiet moments of prayer, where faith remains,

Courage becomes a sanctuary, where healing reigns.

Stay in the fight, through the battles untold,

A patient persists, in courage to behold.

In the shadows of the unknown, where courage will reign,

Stay in the fight through the tears and pain.

TIMING AND GOD'S HEALING

In shadows deep, where courage wanes,

A journey faced through trials and pains.

"Timing and God's Healing," the tale we weave,

For sick and weary hearts, we grieve.

In the stillness of the darkest night,

A flicker of hope, a guiding light.

The clock ticks on, but trust, dear friend,

In the hands of time, your wounds will mend.

Diabetes melilotus's cruel grasp may dim the sun,

Yet within your spirit, battles are won.

Through valleys low and mountains high,

God's healing touch is ever nigh.

In the tapestry of life, a thread unseen,

Woven with purpose, a purpose keen.

For every moment, each breath you take,

Is a step towards the dawn, a step to break.

The hands of time may seem unkind,

Yet miracles unfold, the heart will find.

With patience as your steadfast guide,

A symphony of healing, in God's time, will abide.

Embrace the strength within your soul,

Let faith and courage take control.

For in the ebb and flow of pain,

A brighter dawn, your spirit will regain.

"Timing and God's Healing" in every breath,

A melody of grace, conquering death.

Hold on, dear warrior, to hope's embrace,

For miracles bloom in God's boundless grace.

SURROUNDING MY WILL TO CHRIST

In the hushed corridors of battling strife,

Where shadows linger, and steal the light,

A symphony of strength, in the heart's expanse,

"Surrounding My Will to Christ," the healing dance.

Through the tapestry of trials woven,

Each thread is a story, in pain, unbroken.

With courage as a compass, hope as the guide,

Christ's embrace, a sanctuary inside.

whispers may echo despair,

Yet faith blooms, a flower rare.

In the sacred silence of prayer's embrace,

A divine refuge, a boundless grace.

Oh, weary soul, with every weakening breath,

Know that you're cradled in the arms of faith.

The battle may rage, the night may be long,

Yet in surrender to Christ, you grow strong.

Let the warmth of love be your soothing balm,

As Christ's healing touch brings a calming calm.

For in the depths of struggle, the spirit's rebirth,

"Surrounding My Will to Christ," a testament of worth.

Embrace the courage, let hope prevail,

In Christ's compassion, every fear frail.

Through valleys of pain and mountains of will,

You're surrounded by love, in surrender, be still.

MOUNTAIN IN MY WAY

In the shadowed valley, where echoes of fear reside,

A mountain stands tall, on life's arduous ride.

"Mountain in My Way," daunting and steep,

Yet within your spirit, resilience runs deep.

Arthritis's tempest may rage, a relentless storm,

But within your core, a warrior is born.

Each step uphill, a triumph in the face,

Of the mountainous challenge, an unyielding grace.

The peak may seem distant, obscured by pain,

Yet strength blossoms, like flowers after rain.

"Mountain in My Way," an obstacle to climb,

Yet courage within you, transcends space and time.

Breathe in the winds of hope, let them carry you high,

As you ascend the slopes beneath the sky.

In the face of adversity, a spirit unswayed,

A determination, like sunlight, cannot be dimmed or frayed.

See, the summit awaits with a triumphant view,

A testament to the strength residing in you.

"Mountain in My Way," a chapter to overcome,

With each step, a victory, with each breath, a drum.

Hold on, dear warrior, let hope be your guide,

For on the other side, healing resides.

The mountain may stand, but so do you,

A testament of courage, strength and true.

HEALING POWER OF CHRIST

In the quiet chambers where shadows dwell,

A whispered prayer, a story to tell.

"Healing Power of Christ," a soothing balm,

In the heart's sanctuary, a comforting psalm.

illness grasp may tighten its hold,

Yet in Christ's embrace, your spirit unfolds.

A healer divine, with arms outstretched wide,

Guiding you through the ebb of the tide.

With every ache and every pain,

Feel Christ's presence, a gentle rain.

Through valleys of fear and mountains of despair,

His healing touch, an answer to prayer.

In the tapestry of trials, a thread of faith,

A beacon in darkness, dispelling all wraith.

"Healing Power of Christ," a sacred flame,

Igniting hope, rekindling the game.

Let the warmth of grace envelop your soul,

In Christ's love, find yourself whole.

For in surrender to the divine light,

Miracles bloom, dispelling the night.

Hold on, dear one, to the promise of morn,

In Christ's healing, a new day is born.

The journey may be tough, the path winding and long,

But with faith as your guide, you emerge strong.

SEEKING ANSWERS

In the quiet spaces where questions reside,

A heart in turmoil, on a challenging tide.

"Seeking Answers," in the whispers of the wind,

A journey of courage, where strength is thinned.

sickness riddle, a puzzle untold,

Yet within your spirit, resilience unfolds.

Through the maze of uncertainty, a steadfast quest,

Seeking answers, finding solace in unrest.

In the silence, hear the rhythm of your breath,

A melody of hope, conquering the depth.

The road may wind, and shadows may dance,

Yet within your spirit, a resilient stance.

Questions may linger, like shadows in the night,

But each step forward is a beacon of light.

"Seeking Answers," an anthem of grace,

A testament to courage, in this challenging space.

Hold on, dear one, to the strength within,

For healing begins where hope has been.

In the vast unknown, find a sacred trust,

A solace in faith, a refuge that's just.

The answers may unfold like petals in spring,

In the garden of time, where miracles sing.

"Seeking Answers," a pilgrimage through fear,

Yet within your spirit, hope draws near.

HEALING WATERS

In the depths of ailment, where shadows loom,

A quest for solace, a healing cocoon.

"Healing Waters," a sanctuary profound,

In the ebb and flow, where grace is found.

Pain tempest, a turbulent sea,

Yet within your spirit, a resilient glee.

Beneath the surface, where strength aligns,

"Healing Waters," where hope defines.

Let the waves of courage kiss your shore,

As you navigate the unknown, seeking more.

In the healing waters, a sacred refrain,

A melody of peace that counters the pain.

Feel the current of faith, serene and wide,

As healing waters cradle you inside.

"Healing Waters," a haven to explore,

A balm for wounds, a tranquil shore.

In the dance of reflections, find your grace,

As serenity washes over, leaving its trace.

Through the healing waters, an embrace divine,

A sanctuary where your spirit will shine.

Hold on, dear one, to the gentle stream,

For within its depths, dreams are redeemed.

In the rhythm of hope, let your heart be led,

"Healing Waters" whispering, you're not alone, be steady.

HOLD ME JESUS AND EASE MY FEARS

In the quiet hours of the darkest night,

Where illness casts shadows, and hope takes flight,

"Hold Me, Jesus, and Ease My Fears," a prayer,

Whispered on lips burdened with despair.

storm may rage, relentless and strong,

Yet in faith's refuge, you truly belong.

With trembling hands and a heart heavy with tears,

Reach out to Jesus to calm your fears.

In the gentle embrace of the Savior's love,

Find solace below, find strength from above.

"Hold Me, Jesus," let the healing begin,

A sacred dance, where faith and courage twin.

As pain weaves its story, and shadows entwine,

Let the arms of Jesus be where you recline.

In the stillness of grace, find a quiet retreat,

Where fear and affliction in love may meet.

Hold on, dear soul, to the anchor of hope,

In Jesus' arms, find the strength to cope.

For in the valleys of illness, in the midst of tears,

His love whispers, "Hold Me, and Ease Your Fears."

So, cling to the promise of a brighter dawn,

Where the healing touch of Jesus is drawn.

In the tender shelter of His divine embrace,

May love, hope, and grace mark your journey.

LIVING THROUGH THE PAIN ONE DAY AT A TIME

In the labyrinth of suffering, where shadows creep,

A journey marked by pain, yet courage runs deep.

"Living Through the Pain, One Day at a Time," the anthem,

For the brave hearts wrestling with an affliction's tandem.

Malaria's grip may tighten, a relentless hold,

Yet within your spirit, resilience unfolds.

Through the relentless storm, a determined climb,

Living through the pain, one day at a time.

Each sunrise, a testament to your strength,

A symphony of hope, where shadows relent.

In the tapestry of struggle, find a rhyme,

As you navigate through pain, one day at a time.

Let the breaths you take be a victory song,

In the melody of survival, you belong.

"Living Through the Pain," a resilient chime,

As you face the challenges, one day at a time.

Hold on, dear warrior, to the moments of grace,

In the struggle, find a sacred space.

For in the midst of turmoil, a spirit can climb,

Living through the pain, embracing one day at a time.

WAITING ON THE LORD

In the hush of the hospital, where time stands still,

A patient heart beats, an unwavering will.

"Waiting on the Lord," a quiet refrain,

A journey through illness, marked by patience and pain.

Dengue fever's shadows may cast a daunting shade,

Yet in the waiting, faith does not fade.

Through the silence, let hope be stirred,

For in patience's embrace, strength is conferred.

The clock may tick with an uncertain sound,

Yet in the waiting room, grace is found.

"Waiting on the Lord," a sacred space,

A testament of trust, a resilient embrace.

In the corridors of uncertainty, find your peace,

Let worries and fears in the stillness decrease.

For the hands of the Healer move with accord,

As you navigate through waiting, waiting on the Lord.

Hold on, dear one, to the promises untold,

In the waiting, let your spirit unfold.

For in the pauses, in the quiet accord,

Find solace and strength, waiting on the Lord.

In the tapestry of time, let patience be your guide,

As you navigate through the ebb and tide.

"Waiting on the Lord," a testament to endure,

In the waiting, find healing, find a cure.

NOTHING BUT GOD

In the silence of struggle, where shadows cast their veil,

A spirit undeterred, a heart that won't frail.

"Nothing but God," a mantra in the darkest night,

A beacon of hope, a source of endless light.

Mental illness's grip may tighten, a relentless foe,

Yet in the Divine's embrace, strength does grow.

In the depths of despair, when hope seems flawed,

Trust in the journey, in nothing but God.

Through the valleys of pain, and mountains of fear,

Feel the comforting presence, drawing near.

"Nothing but God," a whispered prayer,

An affirmation of grace, in the healing air.

When the road seems long, and the burden feels heavy,

Lean on the eternal, on God's embrace steady.

In the tapestry of suffering, in the paths untrod,

Find solace and peace, in nothing but God.

Hold on, dear one, to the faith deep inside,

In the vastness of His love, let fear subside.

For during affliction, when odds may seem odd,

Discover strength and resilience, in nothing but God.

FAMILY IS EVERYTHING

In the realm of illness, where shadows may loom,

A tapestry of love, weaving through the gloom.

"Family is Everything," the sacred song,

A melody of support, where hearts belong.

Bipolar disorder's whispers may echo, a daunting sound,

Yet within the family circle, strength is found.

Through the trials and the pain that life may bring,

Hold on, dear one, for family is everything.

In the warmth of embraces, healing begins,

A collective strength that adversity thins.

With every step, with every challenging fling,

Find solace and courage, for family is everything.

Through the tests, the treatments, and the tears,

Family's love transcends all fears.

"Family is Everything," a resounding theme,

A fortress of support, like a comforting dream.

Hold on to the laughter that echoes in your home,

In the unity of love, you're never alone.

Through the uncertainty that illness may bring,

Find resilience and hope, for family is everything.

In the quiet spaces, in the noisy din,

Know that love's healing touch is akin.

"Family is Everything," a mantra to sing,

A source of strength, where hearts take wing.

CHRIST SACRIFICE

In the heart's chapel, where shadows dance,

A patient soul in a sacred trance.

"Christ's Sacrifice," a hymn of grace,

In the sanctuary of illness, a healing embrace.

Stroke's presence, a tempest's roar,

Yet within, a spirit to explore.

In the echoes of pain, a whispering plea,

For Christ's sacrifice to set the spirit free.

Through the valleys of despair, Christ walks,

His love transcending the toughest talks.

In the crucible of suffering, a sacred price,

A healing balm in Christ's sacrifice.

Feel His presence in each labored breath,

A symphony of love, stronger than death.

"Christ's Sacrifice," a beacon of light,

Guiding the soul through the darkest night.

Hold on, dear one, to the nails scarred hands,

As Christ's love across the spirit expands.

In the journey of affliction, a sacred device,

A promise of comfort in Christ's sacrifice.

Let the wounds of the heart find their mend,

In the shadow of the cross, love extends.

"Christ's Sacrifice," a sanctuary sublime,

During trials, an enduring rhyme.

HEAVEN

In the shadows of illness, where courage is tried,

A journey unfolds, where hope is our guide.

"Heaven," a beacon beyond the pain and despair,

A promise whispered, a solace to share.

Epilepsy's tempest may rage, storms may assail,

Yet within your spirit, a resilient sail.

Through the storms and the night that seems never to wane,

"Heaven" beckons, where healing begins again.

In the tapestry of time, each thread a prayer,

"Heaven" weaves a love that's beyond compare.

For every tear shed and every weary plea,

A step closer to the place where souls roam free.

Hold on, dear one, to the whispers of grace,

In the sanctuary of hope, find a resting place.

Through the valleys of struggle, the mountains so steep,

"Heaven" awaits, where your spirit finds keep.

In the quiet moments, when strength is withdrawn,

Let the promise of "Heaven" be a comforting dawn.

For beyond the trials, beyond what we can see,

"Heaven" holds the promise of eternity.

So, in the echoes of pain and the silence between,

Find solace, find peace, in the unseen.

"Heaven," a melody where healing streams,

In the heart's refuge, where hope gleams.

WALKING WITH GOD

In the depths of ailment, where shadows entwine,

A journey unfolds, where the heart aligns.

"Walking with God," a sacred stride,

Through the valleys of sickness, where faith resides.

Osteoporosis's whispers may echo with fear,

Yet in the divine companionship, courage draws near.

With every step, in each trial faced,

"Walking with God," in His love embraced.

In the silence of suffering, find peace profound,

As God's presence echoes without a sound.

Through the pain, where tears may trod,

Take comfort in "Walking with God."

Hold on, dear one, to the hands unseen,

Guiding you through what might have been.

In the tapestry of trials, a path gently trod,

In the company of heaven, "Walking with God."

In the quiet moments and the restless nights,

Feel the warmth of grace, reaching new heights.

For in the journey, where the unknown is trod,

Find strength, find peace, "Walking with God."

So, with each breath, let faith be your guide,

In the company of the divine, you confide.

In the symphony of life, where trials may prod,

Take heart, find courage, "Walking with God."

THE RIGHT HAND OF CHRIST

In the valley of affliction, where shadows linger near,

A spirit in turmoil, holding onto fear.

"The Right Hand of Christ," a promise to embrace,

Guiding through the struggle, a comforting grace.

disease's tempest may howl, a relentless storm,

Yet in the refuge of Christ's right hand, transform.

With each painful step, with each weary plight,

Feel the solace in His grasp, holding you tight.

Through the maze of uncertainty, where doubts may loom,

"The Right Hand of Christ," dispelling the gloom.

In the tapestry of trials, let His love be unfurled,

A sanctuary of peace in the tumultuous world.

Hold on, dear one, to the hands that never part,

In the right hand of Christ, find strength to restart.

In the silent moments, in the darkest hour,

Feel His healing touch, like a delicate flower.

For in the promise of His ever-present might,

"The Right Hand of Christ" leads to a hopeful light.

Through the valleys of illness, the mountains climbed,

In His embrace, find comfort, transcending time.

So, let your heart lean on the Savior's hand,

In His love, in His grace, firmly stand.

"The Right Hand of Christ," a promise never to depart,

Guiding, comforting, healing the wounded heart.

I AM

I am strong, a resilient flame,

Even when I feel weak, life's a challenging game.

I am whole, though incomplete I may feel,

For the Holy Spirit within me, a presence that's real.

I am His, embraced in the arms divine,

A sacred union, a love that intertwines.

I am, and He is mine, in the tapestry of grace,

A journey of healing, where shadows erase.

I am more than the whispers of illness may convey,

A spirit enduring, finding strength each day.

I am, I am, a declaration of might,

In the heart's sanctuary, where faith takes flight.

I am strong, for His strength is my song,

Even in moments where life feels wrong.

I am whole, a masterpiece in the making,

For in the Creator's hands, there's no forsaking.

I am His, and He is mines,

In the dance of life, where the soul intertwines.

I am a testament to resilience,

For in the I am, find the sacred brilliance.

PRAISING GOD

In the silent chambers of the suffering heart,

Where illness weaves a tapestry, tearing apart.

"Praising God," a hymn amid the aching strife,

A melody of hope, a healing rhythm of life.

Crohn's disease's whispers may echo in the quiet night,

Yet within your spirit, a flame burns bright.

In the symphony of pain, let gratitude unfurl,

"Praising God," a song for every boy and every girl.

With every labored breath, find praise anew,

In the sacred moments, where grace breaks through.

Through the valleys of despair, the mountains steep,

"Praising God," find solace in the promises to keep.

Hold on, dear soul, to the whispers of grace,

In the darkest corners, let gratitude trace.

For in the journey of affliction, where tears may trod,

Discover strength and peace, in praising God.

In the quietude of suffering, let praise ascend,

A sacred chorus, where brokenness may mend.

"Praising God," in the storm, in the calm,

A dance of faith, a soothing healing balm.

So, lift your voice in the face of despair,

"Praising God," let gratitude fill the air.

For in the heart's anthem, where troubles may prod,

Find courage, find comfort, in praising God.

PRAISING GOD THROUGH IT ALL

In the quiet whispers of the hospital halls,

Where pain is a chorus and despair often falls.

"Praising God Through It All," a hymn in the night,

A melody of resilience, a beacon of light.

Ulcerative colitis's shadows may cast a daunting shade,

Yet in the praise, a strength is displayed.

Through the echoing halls, where tears may sprawl,

"Praising God Through It All," healing begins to enthrall.

With each labored breath, a prayer ascends,

In the symphony of suffering, where hope amends.

Through the trials that echo, the mountains tall,

"Praising God Through It All," find solace in the call.

Hold on, dear heart, to the faith that endures,

In the midst of affliction, where hope reassures.

For in the sanctuary of praise, even when tears fall,

Discover courage, find comfort, praising God through it all.

In the quiet moments and the tumultuous strife,

Let gratitude blossom, let praise be life.

"Praising God Through It All," a sacred balm,

A testament of faith, a comforting psalm.

So, lift your voice, let gratitude enthrall,

In the journey of healing, praising God through it all.

MY ANCHOR

In the tempest of illness, where waves may collide,

A spirit navigates, anchored by love inside.

"My Anchor," steadfast in the stormy sea,

A beacon of hope, grounding the soul's esprit.

tumult may roar, a relentless gale,

Yet in your anchor's embrace, courage prevails.

Through the surging waves, in the darkest night,

"My Anchor" holds firm, guiding toward the light.

In the depths of uncertainty, where fears may swim,

Feel the grounding force, your anchor within.

With each trial faced, with every heavy squall,

"My Anchor" steadies, never to let you fall.

Hold on, dear one, to the anchor of grace,

In the turbulent currents, find a safe embrace.

In the silent whispers of your spirit's call,

Discover strength and solace in your anchor overall.

For when the seas of suffering threaten to overwhelm,

"My Anchor" secures, a steadfast realm.

In the dance with illness, where shadows may sprawl,

Hold fast to your anchor, for it won't let you enthrall.

So, in the ebb and flow, in the rise and fall,

Find peace, find strength, in your unwavering "My Anchor" thrall.

JESUS IS STEADY

In the storm of affliction, where waves crash and roar,

A soul seeks solace on an unsteady shore.

"Jesus Is Steady," an anchor in the tempest's might,

A constant presence, a guiding light.

winds may howl with relentless force,

Yet in the arms of Jesus, find a steady course.

Through the tumultuous sea of pain and dread,

"Jesus Is Steady," a refuge where fears are shed.

In the quiet spaces of the suffering heart,

Feel the assurance, where grace imparts.

Through the valleys of despair, the mountains tall,

"Jesus Is Steady," never letting you fall.

Hold on, dear one, to the unchanging hand,

In the tumultuous sea, on the shifting sand.

In the midst of chaos, in the anxious confetti,

Find peace, find strength, for Jesus is steady.

For when the storms threaten to overwhelm,

"Jesus Is Steady," a calming realm.

In the dance with illness, where shadows may sprawl,

Rest secure in the arms of Jesus, for He is steady through it all.

JESUS HAS ALREADY SECURED A PLACE FOR ME

In the labyrinth of illness, where shadows may entwine,

A weary heart seeks solace, a sacred place to find.

"Jesus Has Already Secured a Place for Me," a whispered grace,

A haven in the storm, a promise in embrace.

Endometriosis's whispers may echo with a daunting sound,

Yet in the heart's sanctuary, hope is found.

Through the trials that linger, in the darkest night,

"Jesus Has Already Secured a Place for Me," a guiding light.

In the echoes of pain and the burdens carried high,

Feel the assurance in the Savior's sky.

Through the valleys of despair, where fear may be,

"Jesus Has Already Secured a Place for Me,"

a promise to set the spirit free.

Hold on, dear one, to the unwavering hand,

In the realm of healing, where promises stand.

In the midst of affliction, in the vast eternity,

Find comfort, find strength, for Jesus has secured a place for thee.

For when the journey seems long, and shadows sprawl,

Rest assured, dear soul, Jesus has secured a place for all.

In the tapestry of grace, where love eternally weaves,

Find peace, find solace, in the promise that never leaves.

MY ANCHOR IS SURE WITH A SOLID HOLD

In the ocean of affliction, where tempests unfold,

A weary heart seeks refuge, a story yet untold.

"My Anchor Is Sure with a Solid Hold," a mantra to behold,

A steadfast promise in the storm's fierce cold.

suffering gusts may howl, a relentless might,

Yet in Christ anchor's certainty, I find a guiding light.

Through the rolling waves, in the darkest night,

"My Anchor Is Sure," a beacon burning bright.

In the currents of uncertainty, where fears may roam,

Feel the grounding strength, your anchor at home.

With each trial faced and every tempest rolled,

"My Anchor Is Sure with a Solid Hold."

to the grip so firm,

In the face of adversity, let your spirit affirm.

In the tumultuous sea where challenges unfold,

Find peace, find strength in the anchor's solid hold.

For when the winds threaten to take their toll,

"My Anchor Is Sure," a refuge for the soul.

In the dance with illness, where shadows may be bold,

Rest secure, dear heart, in the anchor's steadfast hold.

FAMILY

In the realm of illness, where shadows may encroach,

A haven of love, a family's unwavering approach.

Through the trials and the tests, a unity unfolds,

"Family," a fortress where strength and solace molds.

Sickle cell anemia's whispers may echo, a challenging refrain,

Yet within the family's embrace, resilience does sustain.

In the tapestry of care, woven stitch by stitch,

"Family," a shelter where spirits enrich.

Through the corridors of worry, where fears may roam,

Feel the warmth of love, an eternal home.

In the heart's healing journey, where hope is extolled,

"Family," a sanctuary in the story yet untold.

Hold on, dear one, to the bonds that never sever,

In the face of adversity, love is the tether.

Through the valleys of sickness, where shadows are scrolled,

Find strength and courage in the arms of "Family" bold.

For when the storm rages and uncertainty takes its toll,

"Family" stands firm, a refuge for the soul.

In the dance with illness, where stories are paroled,

Celebrate the love that resides in "Family," untold.

RUNNING TOWARDS THE CROSS MY SALVATION

In the shadows of affliction, where echoes of pain prevail,

A soul seeks refuge, an unwavering trail.

"Running Towards the Cross, My Salvation," a pilgrimage profound,

A journey of healing, on hallowed ground.

whispers may linger, a somber refrain,

Yet in the pursuit of the cross, find strength to sustain.

Through the trials that echo, in the darkest night,

"Running Towards the Cross," a pathway to light.

In the silence of suffering, let redemption unfold,

As you run towards the cross, where salvation is told.

With each step, feel grace in every stride,

A sanctuary of healing where hope will abide.

Hold on, dear one, to the promise it bestows,

In the shadow of the cross, faith steadily grows.

In the midst of affliction, where fears may enthrall,

Running towards the cross, find salvation in it all.

For in the arms of grace, find solace and peace,

As you run towards the cross, let your faith release.

"Running Towards the Cross, My Salvation," a triumphant call, A
testament of strength, as you rise, stand tall.

HEALING WATERS

In the canvas of affliction, where shadows may dance,

A spirit yearns for solace, for a healing chance.

"Healing Waters," a sanctuary to explore,

A tranquil stream where weary hearts restore.

Hemophilia's tempest may roar with relentless might,

Yet in the healing waters, find strength to fight.

Through the currents of pain, in the darkest night,

"Healing Waters" beckon, a source of respite.

In the ebb and flow of suffering's tide,

Let the healing waters be your guide.

In the whispers of hope that gently cascade,

Find comfort and peace in the serenade.

Hold on to the gentle flow,

Where healing waters compassionately bestow.

In the midst of struggle, where tears may fall,

"Healing Waters" embrace, soothing and tall.

For in the dance with illness, where shadows may play,

Find renewal and strength, let healing waters sway.

Through valleys of despair, where courage falters,

Discover the grace of replenishing healing waters.

WAY MAKER

In the shadows of sickness, where uncertainty may loom,

A heart yearns for light, in the impending gloom.

"Way Maker," a divine architect of the soul,

Crafting paths of courage to make broken spirits whole.

Yet in the melody of faith, a hope is found.

Through the winding trails where despair may play,

"Way Maker" guides with the promise of a brighter day.

In the tapestry of struggle, where threads entwine,

Feel the presence of the Maker, a love divine.

With every labored breath and every weary sigh,

"Way Maker" unfolds pathways where dreams may fly.

The hands that carve the way,

In the intricate design, let your fears allay.

In the midst of affliction, where shadows may accrue,

"Way Maker" opens doors to vistas new.

For when the night seems endless, and hope feels far,

"Way Maker" is the beacon, the guiding star.

In the dance with illness, where shadows may confer,

Trust in the Maker.

So, endure the night, let faith be your stay,

For the Maker of ways paves a hopeful way.

In the echoes of trials, let your spirit partake,

For "Way Maker" is crafting a path for your sake.

SEEKING HIM

In the quiet corridors of illness, where shadows often tread,

A soul seeks peace, where prayers are gently spread.

"Seeking Him," a pilgrimage of the heart,

In the healing journey, a hopeful start.

Yet in the seeking, find a sanctuary.

Through the maze of uncertainty, where fears may swim,

"Seeking Him" unfolds a healing hymn.

In the stillness of prayers and the silence deep,

Feel the presence of comfort, where hope takes a leap.

With each heartbeat, in the rhythm of the soul's whim,

"Seeking Him" becomes a pathway to swim.

Hold on to God's promises untold,

In the seeking, find a refuge to unfold.

In the tapestry of trials, where shadows dim,

Discover strength anew in the act of seeking Him.

For in the sacred spaces where spirits align,

"Seeking Him" unveils a love divine.

In the dance with illness, where the light may seem slim,

Find reassurance, find peace, in the solace of seeking Him.

GOD, I KNOW YOU HEAR ME

In the silence of suffering, where pain takes its toll,

A prayer rises, from the depths of the soul.

"God, I know you hear me," whispered with might,

In the stillness of night, in the absence of light.

heart attack's whispers may echo, a haunting plea,

Yet in the prayer's echo, find strength and glee.

Through the valleys of despair, where shadows dim,

"God, I know you hear me," a heartfelt hymn.

In the sacred dialogue, where faith is professed,

Feel the presence of God, in moments of rest.

With each heartbeat, in the soul's sacred bazaar,

"God, I know you hear me," a peace, a star.

Hope to the assurance untold,

In the echoes of prayer, let your spirit unfold.

In the tapestry of trials, where shadows may spree,

"God, I know you hear me," find strength in decree.

For in the sacred space where spirits commune,

"God, I know you hear me," a comforting tune.

NO TIME TO WASTE

Hold onto the faith, for God hears thee.

In the tapestry of time, where shadows may weave,

A soul grapples with illness, seeking reprieve.

"No Time to Waste," a mantra in the silence profound,

In the urgency of moments, healing is found.

a relentless plea,

Yet in the heartbeat of now, find strength to decree.

Through the corridors of uncertainty, where fears may paste,

"No Time to Waste," embrace life with haste.

In the symphony of breaths, in the rhythm of today,

Feel the pulse of existence, a dance to convey.

With each passing second, a chance to taste,

"No Time to Waste," in love and joy to baste.

In the tapestry of now, where life interlaces,

"No Time to Waste," find courage in the embraces.

For in the journey of today, where shadows recede,

Discover resilience, let your spirit lead.

"No Time to Waste," in the moments you chase,

Live fully, love deeply, for there's no time to waste.

NEW DAY

In the arms of night, where shadows may confide,

A patient soul awaits the dawn, a hopeful guide.

"New Day" whispers softly, a promise to believe,

In the canvas of darkness, where dreams may weave.

Psoriasis's whispers may linger, a somber song,

Yet in the morning light, find strength to be strong.

Through the corridors of pain, where shadows sway,

"New Day" emerges, casting darkness away.

In the first light's kiss, feel renewal's breath,

A symphony of hope, transcending life and death.

With each sunrise, a chance to find your way,

"New Day" beckons, a fresh chapter to assay.

Hold on, dear one, to the dawn's embrace,

In the sunrise, let your spirit find its grace.

In the tapestry of time, where shadows may stray,

"New Day" unfolds, painting a brighter display.

For in the cycle of night and the morning's birth,

"New Day" embodies resilience and worth.

let hope lead the way,

Embrace the dawn, it is a new day.

YESTERDAY IS GONE

In the tapestry of time, where shadows may trace,

A soul confronts illness, seeking solace and grace.

"Yesterday is gone," a mantra whispered with might,

In the canvas of now, find strength to take flight.

a haunting refrain,

Yet in the present moment, let healing reign.

Through the corridors of yesterdays, where shadows persist,

"Yesterday is gone," in today's dawn, find a twist.

In the symphony of memories, where echoes play,

Feel the heartbeat of now, a new rhythm to convey.

With each breath, embrace the chance to rewrite,

"Yesterday is gone," in the day's unfolding light.

Hold on, dear one, to the gift of today,

In the whispers of the wind, find a hopeful say.

In the tapestry of moments, where shadows withdraw,

"Yesterday is gone," embrace the present's thaw.

For in the dance with time, let courage lead,

"Yesterday is gone," sow the seeds.

In the journey of healing, where shadows are withdrawn,

Step into the light, for yesterday is gone.

TODAY WE START FRESH

In the canvas of dawn, where a new day is birthed,

A soul arises, with hope gently unearthed.

"Today We Start Fresh," a mantra to declare,

In the morning's embrace, leave behind despair.

Gout's whispers may linger from the night,

Yet in the sunrise, find strength to take flight.

Through the shadows that trailed in the night's mesh,

"Today We Start Fresh," a chance to refresh.

In the palette of possibilities, where colors blend,

Feel the warmth of a sunrise, a healing trend.

With each breath, embrace the moment's caress,

"Today We Start Fresh," let go of distress.

Hold on, dear one, to the promise untold,

In the morning light, let your spirit unfold.

In the tapestry of a new day, where shadows recess,

"Today We Start Fresh," a journey to progress.

For in the dance with time, find courage anew,

"Today We Start Fresh," a perspective to pursue.

In the symphony of life, where hope coalesces,

Step into the sunlight, for today, we start fresh.

GOD KNOWS BEST

In the heart's quiet chamber, where shadows may dwell,

A soul confronts illness, a tale only time can tell.

"God Knows What Is Best," a whisper in the silence,

In the symphony of healing, where patience finds its balance.

Anemia's echoes may resonate, a daunting sound,

Yet in the divine plan, hope is tightly bound.

Through the corridors of uncertainty, where fear may nest,

"God Knows What Is Best," in His hands, find rest.

In the tapestry of trials, where shadows may play,

Feel the guiding hand, leading the way.

With each prayer uttered, in the soul's earnest quest,

"God Knows What Is Best," let faith manifest.

Hold on, dear one, to the unwavering belief,

In the midst of anguish, find solace and relief.

In the dance with illness, where shadows may invest,

Trust the journey, for God knows what is best.

For when the road seems long, and courage put to test,

"God Knows What Is Best," a comforting jest.

In the cadence of time, where destinies infest,

Find peace, find strength, for God knows what is best.

"BEYOND THE STORM: A POEM OF RESILIENCE"

In the heart's tempest, where shadows dance,

A spirit resilient, ready for the chance.

Beyond the storm, where chaos resides,

A journey unfolds, where hope abides.

Yet within, a strength unbowed.

In the midst of trials, where shadows loom,

Resilience blooms, dispelling the gloom.

Through the thunderous night, where tears may fall,

A symphony of courage, a resilient call.

Beyond the storm, find strength anew,

As the heart whispers, "I will make it through."

Hold on, dear one, to the flicker inside,

In the resilience, let your spirit glide.

Beyond the storm, where the clouds may part,

Find solace and healing in a hopeful heart.

For in the dance with illness, where shadows play,

Resilience becomes a guiding ray.

Beyond the storm, where the sun will rise,

Discover the strength that in you lies.

So endure the night, let your spirit transform,

For beyond the storm, resilience takes form.

In the echoes of struggle, let courage perform,

A poem of resilience, in the heart's reborn.

"WHISPERS OF HEALING: A VERSE FOR THE AFFLICTED"

In the hushed corners of pain, where shadows linger near,

Whispers of healing softly draw near.

A verse for the afflicted, a gentle refrain,

In the tapestry of suffering, a soothing gain.

Affliction whispers may echo with a somber tone,

Yet within the verses of healing, strength is sown.

Through the corridors of anguish, where fears accrue,

Whispers of healing bring comfort anew.

In the silence where tears cascade like rain,

Let the verses of healing ease the ache and pain.

With every breath, with every sigh,

Whispers of healing echo, drawing nigh.

the verses so sweet,

In the healing whispers, find a comforting beat.

I where shadows deceive,

Verses of healing gently interweave.

For when the night seems endless, and shadows tall,

Let the verses of healing gently call.

In the dance with illness, where struggles may entwine,

Find solace, find peace, in the verses divine.

"RADIANCE IN THE SHADOWS: POETIC LIGHT FOR THE ILL"

In the shadows of sickness, where darkness may unfold,

A poetic light emerges, a story to be told.

"Radiance in the Shadows," a beacon so bright,

In the canvas of illness, where courage takes flight.

a relentless sound,

Yet in the poetic light, hope is found.

Through the corridors of despair, where shadows play,

Radiance blooms, guiding the way.

In the verses of resilience, where stanzas unfold,

Feel the warmth of love, a radiance untold.

With each line, with each poetic might,

Radiance in the shadows, a comforting light.

Hold on, dear one, to the verses that sing,

In the poetic light, let your spirit take wing.

In the tapestry of trials, where shadows persist,

Radiance in the shadows, a healing gist.

For when the night seems endless, and hope is frail,

Radiance in the shadows sets sail.

In the dance with illness, where shadows may spill,

Discover strength, find comfort, in the poetic light's thrill.

"EMBRACING GRACE: POETRY FOR THE CANCER WARRIOR"

In the battlefield of illness, where courage is the shield,

A warrior emerges, on the battlefield revealed.

"Embracing Grace," a poetic anthem to declare,

In the midst of the struggle, find strength to bear.

Cancer's whispers may echo, a daunting sound,

Yet in the verses of grace, a warrior is found.

Through the trenches of pain, where shadows play,

Embracing grace becomes the warrior's way.

In the verses that sing of resilience and might,

Feel the armor of grace, woven tight.

With each line, with each poetic trace,

Embracing grace becomes the warrior's embrace.

Hold on, dear warrior, to the verses so bold,

In the battlefield of healing, let your story be told.

In the tapestry of trials, where shadows encase,

Embrace the strength found in poetic grace.

For when the battle is fierce, and hope may sway,

Embracing grace guides the warrior's way.

Discover resilience, find peace, in the poetic grace's unfurl.

In the dance with illness, where shadows may swirl,

"ECHOES OF HOPE: POEMS FOR THE JOURNEY OF RECOVERY"

"Echoes of Hope: Poems for the Journey of Recovery"

In the quiet echoes of healing, where whispers reside,

Poems unfold, a companion for the journey, a comforting guide.

"Echoes of Hope," verses that gently sway,

In the tapestry of recovery, where strength finds its way.

a haunting sound,

Yet in the echoes of hope, resilience is found.

Through the corridors of struggle, where shadows play,

Echoes of hope become a guiding ray.

In the verses of renewal, where stanzas align,

Feel the pulse of recovery, a rhythm so divine.

With each line, with each poetic hue,

Echoes of hope paint the journey anew.

the verses so bright,

In the echoes of hope, find solace and light.

In the tapestry of trials, where shadows may weave,

Echoes of hope gently interleave.

For when the path feels uncertain, and strength may go

Echoes of hope resonate, guiding the journey of recovery's scope. where shadows may swirl, Discover the power, find courage, in the echoes of hope's unfurl.

"SERENITY'S SONG: VERSES FOR THE STRUGGLING SPIRIT"

In the quiet echoes of serenity, where peace may softly sing,

Verses unfold, a balm for the soul, a comforting wing.

"Serenity's Song," a gentle melody to declare,

In the tapestry of struggle, finding solace rare.

whispers may linger, a persistent sound,

Yet in serenity's song, healing is found.

Through the corridors of pain, where shadows may play,

Serenity's verses guide the way.

In the poetry of tranquility, where stanzas align,

Feel the calm of serenity, a refuge divine.

With each line, with each poetic ring,

Serenity's song becomes a soothing spring.

to the verses so serene,

In the echo of serenity, find strength unseen.

In the tapestry of trials, where shadows entwine,

Serenity's song gently intertwines.

For when the heart feels heavy and hope may blur,

Serenity's song whispers, bringing the soul to stir.

In the dance with illness, where shadows may twirl

Discover peace, find resilience, in serenity's gentle swirl

"FROM SHADOWS TO STARS: POETIC INSPIRATIONS FOR THE ILL AT HEART"

In the caverns of darkness, where shadows enthrall,

Poetic inspirations emerge, a beacon for all.

"From Shadows to Stars," verses that softly gleam,

In the tapestry of illness, where dreams redeem.

a somber refrain,

Yet in poetic inspirations, hope ascends again.

Through the valleys of pain, where shadows persist,

From shadows to stars, let inspirations persist.

In the verses of resilience, where stanzas intertwine,

Feel the pulse of inspirations, a symphony so fine.

With each line, with each poetic stride,

From shadows to stars, let inspirations be your guide.

Hold on, dear heart, to the verses that soar,

In the poetry of healing, find strength to explore.

In the tapestry of trials, where shadows may mar,

From shadows to stars, let inspirations set the bar.

For when the night seems endless, and courage may tire,

From shadows to stars, let inspirations inspire.

THE RIGHT HAND OF GOD

In sacred grasp, the Right hand of God still holds,

A touch that comforts, heals, and steers our souls,

With gentle palm that guides us on our way,

And offers solace when we start to stray.

Through valleys deep and mountains steep we go,

This steadfast hand uplifts us, helps us grow,

Yet never forces or constrains our will,

But gently leads with love that's pure and still.

Within this touch lies boundless grace and might,

A source of strength when shadows dim the light,

Compassion flows from every finger's tip,

In every crease, a promise not to slip.

Oh hand divine, in you we find our rest,

With gratitude, we are forever blessed.

Psalms 63:8

8 I cling to you; your right hand upholds me.

www.ingramcontent.com/pod-product-compliance
Lightning Source LLC
Chambersburg PA
CBHW051004140626
46546CB00016B/417

* 9 7 8 1 9 5 5 0 5 0 1 8 0 *